The Ultimate
Book of Wisdom

LaFoy Orlando Thomas III, Esq.

"Knowledge is consciousness of reality. Reality is the sum of the laws that govern nature and of the causes from which they flow." – Ancient Egyptian Proverb

"The half-wise, recognizing the comparative unreality of the universe, imagine that they may defy its laws—such are vain and presumptuous fools, and they are broken against the rocks and torn asunder by the elements by reason of their folly. The truly wise, knowing the nature of the universe, use law against laws; the higher against the lower; and by the art of alchemy transmute that which is undesirable into that which is worthy and thus triumph. Mastery consists not in abnormal dreams, visions and fantastic imaginings or living, but in using the higher forces against the lower-escaping the pains of the lower planes by vibrating on the higher. Transmutation, not presumptuous denial, is the weapon of the master." – The Kybalion

"Man must learn to increase his sense of responsibility and of the fact that everything he does will have its consequences." – Ancient Egyptian Proverb

CONTENTS

CHAPTER 1

INTRODUCTION TO CONSCIOUSNESS: THE EGO AND THE SPIRIT

"When there is no enemy within, the enemies outside cannot hurt you." – African Proverb

Life isn't the time or place to be judgmental. Not life on Earth where we all share human form. We all have a unique collective of strengths, weaknesses, opportunities, and threats. It is my belief that in life we are all destined to have important, cherished relationships with people who possess strengths different from our own and weaknesses that we have to respectfully approach with enduring patience, humility, kindness, and understanding. There will always be people who are both more and less evolved than you are.

In addition to not being able to judge others with completely clean hands, judgments by humans are typically done without the appropriate context. Most things, in fact, are judged without the appropriate context or awareness of the actual cause and effect, which helps me to understand why judging isn't the job of the human being. It appears that only the Most High, or Ultimate Creator as some would say, has all of the relevant facts for any particular situation. A judge presiding over a courtroom, for example, can only hope to be led by the all-knowing spirit within and trust that the laws of the universe will ensure that justice, with the appropriate dose of mercy, is always served.

Some of our greatest trials, tests, and challenges in life will deal with people that we either love or with whom we have important business or social relationships. Whatever the case, life clearly presents a constant set of challenges and how we deal with these challenges individually and collectively will likely determine our state of harmony with ourselves and with the people that we need in this lifetime, the future of our souls, and also the fate of our planet that we appear to unconsciously take for granted.

Recognizing the Enemy Within

Most people who are not too far removed from their right minds wish for harmony in their lives and harmony in their relationships with others. If the ego has been consciously or unconsciously identified with and has overtaken the individual, this person will likely seek something that appears to be the opposite of harmony as judged by behavior. African proverbs have described this concept as having an enemy within and self-observation should provide confirmation of its existence. Those experiencing an enemy within episode have lost, to a large degree, awareness of one's own behavior and the karma-creating effects of such and may need to experience suffering or a stillness intervention in order to return to consciousness.

The ego is a living entity within each of us that secretly seeks to cause pain and disharmony by separating us from the spirit of the Most High that is within us. Since the laws of the universe have demonstrated that when we seek to cause pain in others we also cause pain to ourselves, the intention of the ego is to ultimately destroy the person that it lives within, which is what I believe happened to our beloved Tupac Shakur for example. I'm certain that on at least one occasion that Tupac's spirit instructed him to be at peace, to make peace, and that peace would be brought upon him. However, his ego, or enemy within, was provoked and he proceeded to release energy into the universe which accumulated and created his untimely destruction.

The ego, or enemy within, must not be embraced or identified with in order to prevent it from taking over our being and placing us on a path to cause and receive more pain based on our behavior, which when coupled with the laws of the universe, require us to be served that which we deserve. When a sense of superiority, inferiority, anger, or any form of unhappiness appears, it is likely the enemy within, and it is very important to stay mentally alert of your thoughts, emotions, and actions and to not listen to any music or take in any images, including from the news media, that identify with the negative feelings that have arisen within us.

The Rules of Harmony

In order to have harmony in our daily lives, we must first be present, consciously aware of our thoughts, feelings, actions, vibrations, and surroundings. We must perpetually seek to possess the knowledge of the effects that our actions have on ourselves, society, and the universe as a whole. Harmony cannot be coupled for long with unconsciousness, and ignorance is no excuse.

Harmony is a product of setting and executing good intentions and creating good karma. Without good karma, one cannot consistently experience harmony because when bad karma returns, your harmony shall surely be disturbed. Only once conscious do we have the ability to set good intentions in every area of our lives and to work diligently to become the person required to manifest whatever it is that may be desired.

Returning to Your Spirit

The power that we can obtain and develop when practicing consciousness, which I describe as the art of being present and alert of the earthly and spiritual effects of our thoughts and actions, provides knowledge of our true self as well as the will power to align our actions with the truest source that we've ever known: our spirit, which is our own personal light of life and gift from the Most High. A light of truth and direction.

When we go within and are led by the sprit, all fear leaves the mind and body and one is able to walk confidently with the Most High. When one with the spirit, one is firmly aware that nothing can happen to a person, city, or country that is not first approved of by the Most High. In the face of an enemy, even when outnumbered 1,000 to 1, not one piece of hair on your head may be harmed without permission from the Most High. The only fear that shall remain with someone who is led by their spirit within is fear of what might happen if one is led astray and becomes trapped within the grips of the ego and is unable to be led by their light of life, which is the effect of one's own cause.

Dangers of the Ego: Dancing with the Devil

When we go against the spirit within us, we chose to be led by the ego because we have chosen to make decisions and to pursue a path that the spirit cannot support and we become like sleepwalkers, unable to see or avert the many dangers that are found on the path of the ego. When led by the ego, which can find its beginning with just one bad decision to take action contrary to the voice of our spirits, we are walking in darkness and are bound to stumble, both literally and metaphorically. The spirit attempts to lead us always, but when we go against what the spirit is communicating to us, we allow our egos to convince us that we will be okay doing things another way, which will typically lead to failure, depression, suffering, and, when blessed with another chance, an awakening.

Your ego will cause you to lose people that you love and also cause you to do things that make you worthy of great suffering or death, requiring mercy from the Most High. Whereas confidence, esteem, self-respect, and the giving and receiving of appreciation are good and healthy to the spirit, the ego is a different animal and must be conquered.

The ego is easily offended, which quite often leads to an enemy within experience where the ego shows its true colors. The ego breeds jealousy in self and seeks to breed jealously in others, which is dangerous and often times leads to the suffering or death mentioned above.

Like a disease that pretends to be a friend to the body while it multiplies in size and power, the ego can be a silent enemy within until it believes it is strong enough to kill and destroy both the host and others, which is all the same. For these reasons, I am declaring the ego to be the entity that we know and refer to as Satan the devil.

Assuming it to be a factual story, when Jesus said, "Get from behind me, Satan," after Jesus was tempted to jump from a mountain because he's the son of God and would surely be protected by angels, it is likely that he was speaking to his ego, a voice coming from his own mind which he properly described as Satan.

As a representative of the entity that we know of as Satan the devil, when we choose to take a path or set an intention not consistent with the voice of our spirits, we are in essence asking the ego, the beast that we refer to as the devil, to take a ride with us. And unfortunately, the ride rarely, if ever, ends after the intended singular mission and may continue for days, months, or years, resulting in the need for mercy from the Most High and a new spiritual awakening.

Once in the car with the devil, a person may continue to sing praises to the Lord and even partake in some activities that are considered to be righteous, but don't be fooled. The devil is in control of such a person and will seek to cause havoc at the appointed time. As a liar and a deceiver, the ego works in secret, unknowingly to the host, seeking to kill and destroy.

Some believe that the ego was given to us by the Most High and therefore must serve in some positive capacity. I believe that through a combination of our uncontrollable environments and our misuse of free will, we make decisions that allow the energy that creates the ego to be born, or activated, and to live within us. I don't believe any babies are born with activated egos but they are created and activated within each of us after exposure to energy forces not representative of the Most High.

Operating as the entity that we know as Satan, when our egos are offended, we are then most tempted to speak or act in a way that we later usually describe as devilish. And the more that we feed our egos, the stronger it becomes and the more capable it is to lead us to our own destruction. Therefore, when we feed our egos, we are essentially feeding the entity that we know and refer to as the devil. This entity can also be referred to as our lower self or our dark side.

As a former supporter of gangster rap, I can attest that much of it is ego music as it often times speaks to responding to life's situations in a way that is clearly contrary to our spirits. Observation and self-reflection reveals a rich history of the use of music as a method of conditioning, and it is currently being used to destroy generations of people. By destroy, I mean disconnecting them from their spirits and persuading them to live by the voice of their egos.

I've learned from experience that when we put negative karma into the world consciously it returns with a vengeance, and when we put negative karma into the universe unconsciously it returns just strong enough to hopefully awaken us and get our attention. Therefore, we are always responsible for our own actions, even when done unconsciously, which makes taking guard of what energy forces we allow ourselves to be exposed to of the upmost importance if we wish to live divinely, in peace, and in line with the wishes of the Most High.

Pride: An Extension of the Ego and the Fall of Many

Pride often disguises itself as self-respect but is actually an extension of the ego and is an enemy to the spirit and a blockade preventing many people who are living by the voices of their egos from returning to their spirits.

As self-respect prevents a person from mistreating themselves and from accepting disrespect from others, people filled with pride might actually think they are weak if they show consideration or respect to others. As an extension of the ego, the goal of pride is to destroy the person that it lives within by separating them from their families, causing them to lose their freedom, and, in some cases, bring them to an untimely death that could have been avoided had it not been for their pride.

Although a person with pride may be facing the possibility of becoming homeless, a prideful man or woman may be unwilling to accept a job that the person considers to be beneath him or her. On the other hand, a person with self-respect has too much respect for themselves to become homeless if the situation is avoidable. A person with pride is usually unconscious to the laws of the universe and may often put energy or karma into the universe that a wise person with self-respect would likely be unwilling to intentionally allow to occur because the person knows that all of our actions are karmic in nature.

A wise person with self-respect won't intentionally disrespect someone, even if the person knows that the person that's disrespected has no means by which to retaliate, because a wise person knows that the disrespect will be returned to him or her at some later time or date. To intentionally disrespect someone is to intentionally disrespect yourself because the law of karma will be sure to return the energy that you released into the universe.

Pride causes many people to withhold due apologies, prevent them from admitting error, or from accepting help, and, in some cases, from displaying love and affection to others in the most important or critical of times. Pride is a friend to no one, and a person who is filled with pride should seek to conquer it by means of meditation and prayer to the Most High and then the use of all of your power.

Dealing With the Egos of Others

Although many people, including myself at times, have no interest in catering to the egos of others, it is important to be gentle and tactful when dealing with the egos of others. A person being led by their ego is in a heightened state of sensitivity and can be compared to a person standing at the edge of a high mountain. A push in the wrong direction can send such a person off the edge and into a chaos-creating state of mind where the person begins to unconsciously or uncontrollably put negative energy into the universe that almost always returns to the perpetrator and the intensity of such return typically depends on the level of mercy granted by the Most High. To intentionally do such a thing to a person is the equivalent of doing such a thing to one's self and should be avoided with all thine energy and might.

To intentionally offend the devil in others opens the door for someone to successfully offend the devil in you. The Most High has either created this universe or has allowed for it to be created with a certain set of laws that seek to maintain peace, balance, and order. Harmony comes to those who work diligently to keep harmony with self, others, and the universe, including with nature and with the animals, both large and small.

Befriending Ego Beings

Befriending or dealing with ego beings on a social level is also something not to be taken lightly and caution should be duly exercised. Although life isn't the time or place to be judgmental, one must always observe the surrounding energies and allow the spirit to provide guidance. When someone is living with the sole purpose of feeding the ego, this person becomes extremely dangerous when the ego is bruised and may secretly seek to destroy the person that is held to be responsible for such bruising, which may result from simple activities such as beating the other person in a friendly game or receiving better grades in school than the other person.

Once under the control of the ego and on its mission to destroy, the ego being may seek to rationalize the reasons behind the hate for the other person, which is merely a cover for the fact that the person's ego was bruised and the person has been deceived into believing that the ego is the only thing that the person has to live for.

Since no one person has the strength, wisdom, and discipline to follow his or her spirit 100 percent of the time, we all from time to time fall under the spell of the ego;

however, it is wise to choose friends and business associates who seek alignment with the Most High before all else. Although those seeking alignment with the Most High may fall under the ego and have their egos wounded, such friends and associates are not likely to be persuaded by the ego to carry out prolonged missions of hate, which in essence are missions of self-destruction since hatred causes more damage to the temple that it resides within than it does to any temple that it attempts to obliterate.

The Power to Co-create Your Own Reality

Although I believe that the Most High maintains ultimate authority over our lives and over the universe as a whole, it appears that each of us spirit beings have the power to control, in large part, our realities by controlling our thoughts, feelings, intentions, and our karma, which I describe as a combination of our intentions and how well we have executed on those intentions, whether good or bad. This, I believe, has caused many people to consider themselves to be gods, which depending on the context used may be accurate if meant to infer one's self as a spiritual creator, but in no way should a human ever consider himself to be the equivalent of the Most High.

The harder that we try to live righteously, the louder our spirits speak to us. When we disregard our spirits, the voice turns into a silent whisper until the moment of awakening. Your spirit will lead you to contact to uplift someone at the perfect time when they need it the most. Your ego, on the other hand, will lead you to contact someone and deliver negative energy to them at the worst time in an attempt to give them a heart attack or to derail them from their righteous path, which will usually lead to two-way suffering. There are no coincidences in the universe and careful observation should confirm the validity of these statements.

In conclusion, it is fair to state that I have been introduced to both the Most High and the devil, and the meeting place was inside of me.

CHAPTER 2

GOING WITHIN AND UNVEILING YOUR PERSONAL LIGHT OF LIFE

"Believe nothing, no matter where you read it, or who said it, no matter if I have said it, unless it agrees with your own reason and your own common sense." – Buddha

Silencing the Mind with Meditation

Sitting in a comfortable position, start by taking a deep breath and close your eyes. Be present and quiet. Silence the mind by observing your breathing with undivided attention. When thoughts come to mind, without judgment of the thought, return your focus to your breathing and just listen for at least five minutes and increase the time gradually to a time perfect for the particular occasion. Try not to control your breathing but instead just observe it gracefully.

Although many label this practice as mindful meditation, the mind actually gets a chance to take a breather, recharge, and remove a portion of the effects of the domestication process that we all have inevitably experienced.

Meditation Versus Prayer

Although I believe that prayer to the Most High is of the utmost importance, meditation is just as important. Prayer is without a doubt a very powerful tool, especially when seeking the strength to overcome bad habits or the ability to resist temptation. When we pray, in most cases, we are doing all of the talking and simply communicating things to the Most High that It already knows as it is reasonable to believe that the Most High already knows all. However, when we meditate, we actually stop talking and thinking for a moment and allow the Most High the opportunity to communicate to us, which is what we often need the most.

When many of us pray, we do all of the talking and none of the listening, which doesn't create an opportunity for the Most High to communicate the answers to our problems to us. That's similar to going to the doctor, telling him or her what our symptoms are, and then sticking our fingers into our ears and walking out of the office saying, "blah, blah, blah." I wish not to state that one is more important than the other, but I do wish to state that they are a perfect complement to each other, especially when seeking guidance.

Be True to Thy Spirit, Not Thy Heart or Thy Mind

When seeking to be true to thy spirit, which serves as our internal compass from the Most High, it is important to not confuse the spirit with the heart, which at times will be in alignment with the spirit, but other times it may not. Some believe that the spirit and the heart are the same thing but they are definitely not.

The heart, similar to the mind, can be conditioned, while the spirit will always be in alignment with the Most High. At times, the heart may compel thee to take action that the spirit has clearly directed against. The heart is not always an ally to the righteous, but a tremendous amount of mercy seems to be granted to the person led astray by the heart with good intentions.

For example, the spirit may direct a person to stay clear from another person for reasons not always understood. The heart, however, may compel thee to disregard the spirit due to feelings of love or adoration that can be used to persuade many of men and women alike that their behavior is righteous and approved by the Most High. And since pain and suffering usually follow after disobedience of the spirit, one can quickly learn the voice of the spirit versus the heart or the mind with careful self-observation.

The heart is very powerful and, when combined with the ego, one may be convinced that forbidden behavior done in the name of love will be blessed by the Most High. But don't be deceived. Although mercy from the Most High appears to be enduring and possibly even infinite in nature, it should never be taken for granted or used as a free pass to disobey instruction from the spirit. Suffering shall surely follow after such course of action.

Many people are currently living lives that are inconsistent with their own innate principles, values, and desires that can only be discovered when the mind is silenced and your personal light of life is allowed to shine.

I think we all, when mentally healthy and in touch with our personal light of life, have the ability to determine right from wrong, fair from unjust, and if our behavior is more or less likely to create a return of positive or negative energy vibrations. Energy vibrations are experienced in many forms, some of which are solely in the mind. A bad nightmare that is timely coordinated with improper thought or behavior may be all the universe needs to get your attention. Some may need to experience the nightmare as a reality before the lessons of karma and its effects on harmony become transparent.

I think we all have observed that when we seek to cause disharmony in another person, even if it is just a test of some sort, we have inevitably placed disharmony in our own lives as well. The second hermetic principle, the principle of cause and effect, states that "Every Cause has its Effect; every Effect has its Cause; everything happens according to Law; Chance is but a name for Law not recognized; there are many planes of causation, but nothing escapes the Law."

Once we are aware of our being and the

effects that our thoughts and actions have on ourselves, others, and the planet, we are then conscious and are likely to make decisions that support a healthy mind, body, family and community where human life can continue to survive, thrive, and create. Setting the intention to remain conscious, despite the brutal facts, is of the utmost importance and is just as valuable as the initial intention to become conscious.

The Domestication of the World

It is common for people to become who they have been encouraged to become. A sign that your personal light of life is starting to shine is when you are able to consciously acknowledge that you disagree with the person that you've become and a burning desire to align with your innate values emerges and becomes a driving force for change.

To be able to thoughtfully say that something that you've been practicing most or all of your life is not true to you is a power to be cherished and nourished. Do not take that power for granted once it is possessed. It is a personal awakening and with it comes the ability to identify and become your true self by providing guidance to returning to who you are and distancing yourself from who you've become. As a conscious, independent thinker, outer influences are rightfully cast away in the areas where the spirit should control, such as finding purpose, spiritual beliefs, and the development of a personal code of ethics.

Make it a habit to go within and allow your personal light of life inside of you to provide divine guidance. Many of our most valuable lessons and blessings, both spiritual and material, occur after being true to one's self and following the guided path.

Looking within to answer many of life's toughest questions is the opposite of what many of us have been programmed to do during the domestication process. The first chapter to one of my favorite books, The Four Agreements by Don Miguel Ruiz, does an exceptional job of providing an overview of the domestication process. As children, we enter a world full of opinions, perspectives, and desires that are not our own. Sometimes by way of parental or religious conditioning, or industry and private interest promotion, we accept and adopt these views as our own, many times subconsciously knowing that we are betraying the very essence of our existence.

Subsequently, these beliefs often times become barriers for spiritual growth and inhibit one from reaching and exploring one's true purpose and potential during what is possibly our one and only human experience. It is important to note that whatever a person's purpose is in life, the resources that are required to carry out the task are already within the person and the seeds may only need watering to develop and become fully functional.

Many things, including television and radio programming, religious writings, and the opinions of our parents and friends, contribute to our domestication. Breaking loose from the chains of domestication starts with the basic awareness and acknowledgement that one has been indeed domesticated and transformed, at least in part, into a person that is different from one's true self.

After becoming aware of the effects of your personal domestication, commitment to becoming and remaining conscious in every area of life is required to begin a sustainable journey to true self identification. Once consciousness is present and you arrive at a point where instead of being your thoughts and emotions you are the awareness or observer behind your thoughts and emotions, start to compare the principles, values, and anything else that you've adopted to become the current you to what you truly, deeply feel is your own personal truth.

Many of us have been shamed by society and pressured to hide who we really are in an effort to be compared favorably to the expectations that have been set not by ourselves but from the world that we've joined. I believe it to be a betrayal to one's self to be compelled to carry out an act by your spirit but to not do so because of the laws or expectations of man. Careful consideration should always be given to if the ego is present and encouraging the activity or compulsion. If you are convinced that you are being true to you and that no outside influence is present, I believe that you should act if you believe that doing so would be righteous behavior.

The cure to the virus of external domestication is to decide to be you in your highest form. Take a deep breath, thank the Highest Power for your existence and for all of your many blessings, and get started on your personal journey toward consciousness and unveil, for the world to see, your own personal light of life. I guarantee you that the real you is a much better addition and contribution to the world than your domesticated version could ever dream to be or become. Just remember to go within and do not seek counsel where it cannot be found.

Make-Believe Television

One of the many problems with television programming is its ability to make you believe that life actually works different from actual reality, which causes many people to live and handle situations in manners similar to those seen on screen. This is detrimental because television rarely ever considers the effects of karma, or a return of energy, in the story. Also, when disharmony is caused by external sources, actors or actresses quickly turn to that external source and they attempt to solve the problem externally.

When faced with disharmony, it is an opportunity to look within and recognize the lesson to be learned. In a large majority of cases, the things that bother us are like a mirror showing us the parts of our character that are less evolved and that require attention. To deny that your actions are being mirrored is what *The Kybalion* refers to as presumptuous denial. Presumptuous denial involves refusing to accept what the universe is showing you to be outside the lines of what is acceptable. Transmutation involves going within and changing the formula of your alchemy, which consist of your thoughts, intentions, and deeds.

The Power of Fasting

One of the most physically and spiritually damaging lies taught during the domestication of the world is that breakfast is the most important meal of the day. To break your fast early in the morning takes the opportunity away from your body to use its energy to heal itself as the process of digesting food is rather burdensome for the human body, especially when considering the western diet. The human body was constructed masterfully and has amazing abilities when operated as intended.

Fasting also helps burn fat and helps tremendously with weight control. Although extended fasts are appropriate on occasion, daily fast of at least 16 hours should be the target. For example, if a person finishes dinner at 8:00 PM, the person ideally wouldn't consume anything other than water before noon the following day. If the last meal of the day is finished at 4:00 PM, then 8:00 AM the following day would be a good time to break fast; however, most families in the west are not finishing dinner by 4:00 PM, which makes breakfast a meal that should be consumed on an irregular basis.

In addition to burning fat and promoting self-healing, fasting also promotes self-discipline and the ability to suppress impulsive behavior and the need for instant gratification. When a person is perpetually in a fed state, he or she is constantly satisfying the desires of the flesh, which often leads to the inability to resist other temptations that may appear to be satisfying to the flesh. Also, living in a state of instant gratification often causes one to have anxiety for the future, which makes it difficult to live patiently and joyfully in the present moment.

When the focus is physical health and weight loss, fasting while only consuming water or grape juice is ideal. However, when the objective of fasting is to promote spiritual growth, foregoing food, water, and sex is ideal as the person foregoing food, water, and sex is completely denying the flesh of its natural desires. Rejecting the flesh strengthens the human connection to the spirit within, which is the ultimate goal as the spirit within provides the pathway to our personal salvation from the pains of the lower vibrations of the universe.

Fasting from Social Media

There are many positive aspects to social media platforms, such as when you use them to network, promote your product or service, or bring social awareness to a worthy cause. However, social media requires constant fasting from as well. One of the downsides to social media is the constant flood of unfiltered energy from your social media community. It is important to protect your subconscious mind from energy that is not likely to manifest in a desired manner. In addition to feeding the conscious and subconscious minds with various ideas that may not align with the recipient's true self and purpose, social media is also likely to lead to comparison and judgment, both of which tend to lower individual vibrations and cause unnecessary self-doubt.

Overcoming the Pitfall of Deception

When one intentionally deceives another by words, actions, or omission, the person invites deception to be returned as the laws of the universe require. When a person is a victim to the deception of another, he or she becomes under a spell and gains a false perception of reality and, therefore, becomes easier to control. This false perception of reality pertains to more than just the lie which has been believed and stretches to encompass how one perceives the entire universe, its laws, and the person's true purpose during this lifetime as determined by the Creator.

Being under the deception and spell of another leads to the mental and spiritual degradation of the victim, causing deception to be one of the most malicious acts that can be performed. Much of the world is under a spell and the perpetrators are many, which include governments, corporations, religions, secret societies, and other human beings. Seeking righteousness, enlightenment, and alignment with the Creator returns you to your spirit and in alignment with natural law.

CHAPTER 3

THE ROAD TO CONSISTENT HAPPINESS

"Happiness does not depend on what you have or who you are. It solely relies on what you think." – Buddha

The way that we feel determines a lot in life. I have learned, from the advice of others and then confirmed by careful observation, that the better we feel and the higher the vibrations that we put into the universe the more positive the people, opportunities, circumstances, and ideas are that we will encounter on our path.

Taking Responsibility for Your Own Happiness

For many, maintaining a sense of happiness and wellbeing is dependent on external forces, such as the treatment from spouses, children, parents, friends, employers, and so forth. Those practicing consciousness are able to take control of their minds and dictate the exact feeling that is desired. Although we all may still experience moments of unconsciousness, the more we practice consciousness the less we are likely to be affected by lengthy periods of unconsciousness.

We are all ultimately responsible for maintaining our own sense of happiness and must make a daily effort to attain a joyful spirit that shines through. A conscious, positive mind combined with a spirt of love, peace, and harmony is both contagious and transformative and will create a karmic return matching its vibration as the laws of the universe require.

Practicing consciousness makes one aware more quickly of one's own thoughts and feelings before they are allowed to become identified with and overtake the individual completely.

The Law of Balance

One of the most disregarded universal laws is the law of balance. Although many people believe that maintaining a balanced lifestyle is important, many people don't understand that it is actually a universal law. Some people believe that they may live their lives however they please, which often leads to a misuse of free will.

In many societies across the world, people are encouraged to spend close to, or more than, 100 hours weekly working for money or building businesses and are also persuaded to neglect a variety of essential duties that we all have. Although all people have their own personal journeys and assignments in life that require distinct focuses, we all have a similar set of duties that must be fulfilled to stay in alignment spiritually, mentally, emotionally, and physically.

For example, we all generally have a duty to spend time with and to add value to our families and friends. We must balance that with taking care of our homes and nourishing our minds, bodies, and our spirits. One of our most important duties is to identify our true purposes in life so that we may know the ways in which we are required to add value to society as a whole or, at a minimum, our individual communities. Time and energy must also be dedicated to restoring our relationships with the Most High, which is often damaged by the various energetic forces of society. Although discipline is very important to a person's development, it is important to not become so disciplined that your body or spirit can't effectively communicate what it needs from you.

As with any universal law, when the law of balance is violated, the violator often faces some form of disharmony that is often meant to serve as a spiritual wake-up call. When the law of balance is consistently disregarded, bodily health and inner peace are often compromised along with the health of our family relationships, our relationships with the Most High, and our financial stability. Spiritual wake-up calls have no specific design and have a tendency to come in many forms.

Practicing Positive Self-Talk

Considering that our thoughts are a key component to our happiness, it is important to plant the proper seeds that are likely to grow into happy thoughts. Telling yourself that you are beautiful, happy, healthy, secure, wealthy, positive, spiritually balanced, and a loving person are all great places to start. If you wish to live a life of travel, telling yourself that you will soon be flying all over the world having fun with friends and family is a great idea as well. It is common knowledge that the subconscious mind is a horrible master but a faithful servant. The seeds that we plant into our subconscious minds are likely to manifest in some form whether we truly want them to or not. So it is important to be kind to yourself and practice only planting seeds that are likely to lead to the life that you wish to experience.

Doing Things that You Enjoy

As long as you are not intentionally or negligently hurting anyone or the planet, it is important to maintain a lifestyle that consist of doing the things that you enjoy the most. Especially for those who are extremely hardworking, maintaining a healthy balance is of the utmost importance. Not doing the things that you enjoy will often lead to a spiritual and mental imbalance, which often leads to both emotional and then physical problems.

Exercising for Happiness

Many people exercise to lose weight or to improve their overall health. In addition to exercising for an optimal physical state, many people have discovered the pure happiness that comes from working up a good sweat. For me, running for an extended period of time induces me into a state of euphoria and a sense of accomplishment. After a long run, I feel more confident, energetic, highly motivated, and my attitude in general is much more positive. The key is to find an exercise or set of exercises that provide both the desired health benefits as well as the induced state of euphoria. If you are new to exercising, I recommend starting with a light workout and increasing the intensity and duration gradually. If a beginner starts with an overly intense workout, he or she is likely to either have an injury or encounter extreme soreness, which discourages many novices from continuing on the path to physical fitness.

Ending Chronic Worrying

Stopping the persistent habit of worrying or negative thinking is one of the most challenging aspects of developing our level of emotional intelligence, which I believe is required to achieve advanced levels of spiritual maturity. Observation has confirmed that more times than not, the answers that we seek are often unveiled to us when the mind is still and free of concern or worry, which makes the act of worrying futile and often times counterproductive. Stopping negative thoughts when they first arise is critical as that is when they are at their weakest. The practice of meditation strengthens the muscle that is required to remove the mind's focus from unwanted thoughts. Although weak initially, the muscle shall strengthen gradually as determined by meditation habits coupled with karmic vibrations.

Awareness of the fact that our actions create karmic vibrations, conscious movement throughout life will create a life where there is not much to worry about on a personal level, and the developed mental muscle can quickly move the mind away from any negative thinking and simply focus on observing one's own breathing and on being present in the actual moment. Thus being granted, or blessed, with the ability and opportunity to enjoy life.

Think Before Praying

Many people, including myself, have made specific prayer requests without considering the events that may have to transpire in order for our prayers to be fulfilled. For example, for years I prayed for more strength not realizing that the Most High wouldn't just pour it into my body while I was sleeping or instantly while I was praying. Although that was my desired method for the Most High to answer my prayer, it wasn't realistic. I realized that the Most High doesn't work that way, although in an emergency situation the greatest of miracles may be performed with obvious divine intervention.

Just like if a man prayed for more physical strength, the Most High isn't likely to deliver muscles to the person during the middle of the night. However, the Most High may provide the financial resources for the man to acquire a gym membership or may even provide the man with motivation to exercise to build the desired physical strength.

When praying for mental, emotional, or spiritual strength, the person praying should expect to encounter challenges that provide the opportunities to build and develop the requested strength. A person who constantly prays for strength shouldn't expect an easy life that is free of obstacles, tests, and often some form of disharmony. Mental, emotional, and spiritual strength, just like physical strength, is gained by adding heavier weight to the load being carried. At some point, it becomes wise to take a break from praying for strength and instead to respectfully ask that you are able to recognize and utilize the strength that you already have within you. Most of us don't realize how strong we already are and, in the event that something that appears too heavy to bear does emerge, that our faith combined with the ability of the Most High is sufficient to see us through.

Developing Faith

Faith is one of the most important components to maintaining harmony and staying in alignment when opportunities arise that are tempting, but outside of our alignment. Faith allows you to believe that everything will be okay and that there's a power that is greater than yourself that you may call upon. Believing in this higher power humbles you and, if wise, causes you to seek and submit to Its will.

Seeking alignment with the Most High gives you confidence that your actions have created great favor, protection, and a connection to the infinite resources of the universe. Therefore, seeking and working toward righteousness creates faith. Also, faith is created by calling on that higher power in times of need and giving credit to the Most High when you are allowed to return to a state of harmony.

Without faith, in addition to feeling alone in times of trouble, a person is likely to be a lot more selfish since they don't have the confidence that all of their needs will be fulfilled. Also, without faith, a person is a lot more likely to unconsciously create since faith is often required to even believe in universal law and order. If you are lacking faith, ask for it in prayer and then take advantage when opportunities arise to allow you to develop that faith.

Karma Cleanse

Often times, we as human beings find ourselves in stressful situations where peace appears impossible to obtain. Sometimes, when we become unconscious, we allow our negative karma to accumulate, which eventually smacks us in the face and destroys our happiness and our ability to focus and achieve in life. Not knowing how to overcome this sort of grief is commonplace among many in our society.

The key to overcoming such situations is what I refer to as a karma cleanse. A karma cleanse requires the person to first accept the fact that whatever the person is struggling through is a result of his or her own karma. Accepting responsibility for our hardships is of the utmost importance when seeking to return to a peaceful state of mind. Accepting responsibility for your own karma also allows the required lesson to be learned, which appears to be a prerequisite for returning to peace in a timely manner.

Next I recommend letting go of any hard feelings that you may have against anyone and to treat whatever ill that has happened to you as a creation of your own karma. Life can be compared to a lucid dream that has laws that require us to be served that which we deserve and the power to co-create our own realities.

After clearing your heart of negative feelings and accepting responsibility for your own karma, I recommend staying conscious and spiritually aware of your thoughts, intentions, actions, and the events that we encounter. It is important to try your best to not put any negative energy into the universe and to reduce or eliminate exposing yourself to negative vibrations, including from the news media, scary or violent movies, and negative music. It is equally important to not put any bad energy into the universe and to protect your karma with all of your strength, which means no stealing, no gossiping, no hurting others negligently or intentionally, and trying your best to protect the planet. After completing a karma cleanse with sincere intention of maintaining a righteous lifestyle, peace comes in quick order and stays for as long as we maintain our good karma, consciousness, and high vibration.

The Importance of Cleanliness

There appears to be a connection between cleanliness and the capacity for divine alignment. A clean living environment allows positive energy to circulate freely throughout the home, while a dirty home appears to attract negative energy and often contributes to a lack of mental clarity, emotional uncertainty, and less than harmonious relationships among the occupants.

Both spiritual revelations and ideas for wealth creation come much more abundantly when the home, the mind, the gut, the outer body, and the hands of the person are kept clean. Therefore, in addition to cleaning our homes, it is important to eat clean foods, keep good hygiene, and monitor the mind and avoid negative, or faithless, thinking.

Perceiving the Outer World

When perceiving the outer world, I believe it is important to become conscious of some negative news of events or circumstances throughout the world for the sake of encouraging change. However, I believe it is more important to monitor how much negativity is taken into both the conscious and subconscious minds and to protect your energy field by focusing on as much positivity as possible. The way you feel determines a lot in life. Focusing on too much negativity will inevitably cause you to be overtaken by a chain reaction of negative thoughts, feelings, and events that match. Careful observation should provide personal confirmation.

The powers that be of the current world appear to be in alignment with an energy force that is in opposition to the Most High. Although they are fighting a battle that they will ultimately lose, the current powers that be are defiant and determined to put forth a worthy fight, and no expense is being spared trying to accomplish its ultimate mission of compelling the Most High to allow for the planet, including the righteous that are among us, to be destroyed. Therefore, most music, movies, television series, the news media, and even most tap water supplies are all designed and in place to cause you to lose touch with reality and to perpetually suffer from bouts of misery and self-destruction.

Separating the righteous, whom I describe as those who are seeking alignment with the Most High, from their spirits is the number one tactic of those in opposition to the Most High and prayer, meditation, and careful observation should provide confirmation of such fact. Please do not be deceived. Those in control of this world are not on your side if you are seeking righteousness and such people will intentionally take action to destroy you while smiling and professing to be in the business of doing good and of benefiting society.

It is important to note that there are many that are righteous from various backgrounds. For example, there are Christians with good intentions who have accepted Jesus Christ as their lord and savior because they believe that is how to attain alignment with the Most High. Similarly, there are good-intentioned

Muslims who follow the teachings of Muhammad and the Quran because they believe that is the path to alignment with the Most High. There are some who are good intentioned from the Jewish faith that believe that following the laws of Moses and the Torah are how to attain alignment with the Most High.

The Most High has many followers that are seeking alignment and have the ability to listen to and follow their spirits day and night. However, when a choice is required between following one's own spirit or the text of a particular religious doctrine, in many cases the righteous will disregard their spirits and follow their doctrines, not realizing that the Most High has provided each and every one of us with an internal compass that was meant to serve as the ultimate guide to living in accordance with Its will.

This world is very dark and dangerous at its lowest vibration, and intentionally stepping out of alignment with the Most High exposes one to the will of the entity that we know and refer to as Satan, which in essence is the entity that we know and refer to as the ego, which is the cause of all hate, jealousy, and all forms of unrighteousness.

Beware of Energy Vampires

Living in the ego is a very empty lifestyle. Although there is usually some level of satisfaction when the ego is being fed, once the meal is complete, the person living to satisfy the ego returns to a feeling of emptiness and incompleteness requiring more food for the ego or the capturing of energy from someone seeking to live in the spirit. These people often struggle maintaining an attitude of gratitude and are often never content with their many blessings.

Those of us who are seeking to live in the spirit and according to our purposes often have lots of life energy, which radiates and makes itself known. Those living in the ego are often low energy beings unless food for the ego is perpetual. Those of us living in the spirit have this energy in order to do our Father's work, not to be depleted by or given to ego beings who are causing the earth much destruction with their self-centered approach to life. The enemy of the Most High uses his beings to suck the life from spirit beings to hinder their efforts or even cripple them from being able to do the work that they were destined to complete to improve the world.

Seeking alignment with the Most High

gives a person a life force that is enviable to observers who live by the ego, meaning those who are living to satisfy self without regard to the will of the Most High. Ego beings often deploy various tactics to capture the energy of spirit beings, including starting fights, tempting them to live or take action contrary to their spirits, and very often by diverting the other person's focus away from our Father's tasks and unto them by any means necessary.

It is very important to be aware of the fact that a being living to satisfy the ego and not the Most High will employ these tactics when there is no ego food around, which will likely leave you drained of energy and temporarily feeling defeated for the day.

Even after eliminating toxic people form our lives we tend to think about them and the damage that we may have allowed them to cause, which leads to even more damage to our mental, emotional, physical, and spiritual health. If a person decides that another person is too toxic to have a presence in his or her life, it should also be decided that the toxic person shouldn't be allowed in his or her mind either. Spending time thinking about people or events that destroy your happiness prolongs the suffering that the people or events may have caused and is a form of self-abuse. As previously stated, the more that a person meditates, the more mental strength and control he or she is likely to have over his or her thinking and ability to change unwanted thoughts.

Choosing Mates Based on Spiritual Foundation

There are many people who believe that their spouse has the duty to give them the level of inner peace and joy that only comes from having a solid spiritual foundation and a committed relationship to the Most High. In believing that it is their mate's duty, a debilitating strain is usually placed on the spouse because he or she has been tasked with the impossible. Not many things in life are impossible, but replacing the surreal feeling of happiness and joy that comes from a humble and submissive relationship with the Most High is one that cannot be replicated by man.

Wishing to circumvent the spiritual foundation that is required is a silly act of foolishness and cannot lead to lasting happiness, although one may be deceived for a moment. A person cannot violate the laws of the universe and then bend it to his or her will. The universe has been created to do the bending and suffering shall surely come to the man or woman who seeks to behave without care of consequences or awareness to the true effects of his or her actions. Therefore, it is of the essence to find a mate who is spiritually grounded and has a healthy level of fear or respect for the Most High and universal law. A spiritually grounded pair has the ability to be blessed beyond measure.

A Note to Husbands

One of the most challenging and important duties that men have is the requirement to remain kind to our wives regardless of their attitudes, which includes their thoughts, feelings, and actions. When the wife of a man who seeks righteousness goes unconscious and begins to act in a less-than-desirable manner, it is of the utmost importance for the man to patiently remain conscious and kind.

This does not mean that a man should tolerate disrespect because all people should always firmly assert their right to be respected; however, it does mean that a man who has submitted to the Most High must remain conscious, calm, and kindly embrace his wife when she returns to consciousness. In many instances, by the time that the wife has returned to consciousness, the man has gone unconscious himself and is unable to reestablish harmony when the opportunity presents itself.

In order to remain conscious and kind regardless of the situation, it is important to keep in mind that many times the energy that our spouses direct toward us is a reflection of the energy that we ourselves have released into the universe with our thoughts, feelings, intentions, and deeds. Also, we have all suffered, to some degree, a collection of atrocities and sometimes mentally and emotionally debilitating circumstances, which often starts with childhood experiences. With that said, empathy, which is putting yourself in another person's shoes, will provide critical understanding that is necessary to maintain harmony within the family structure.

A Note to Wives

My personal belief is that a woman should only marry a man that she has the utmost respect for and for whom she has, to some degree, unconditional love. If a woman has a husband who seeks to be righteous and one who has humbly submitted to the Most High, assuming that he also treats her and others fairly and with respect, she should honor him as a king in the same way that he honors her as a queen.

Restoring the Honor of the Woman

Considering that every human being, both male and female, was carried and cared for by a woman before and often times after birth, it makes sense that women should be revered and protected by other females and by the entire male specie as well. No person may enter the planet without consent and carriage by a woman.

Despite the magnificence of a woman, and in many cases because of it, a great deal of effort has been expended minimizing the importance of the woman, which has caused a challenging and less-than-ideal dynamic amongst females, within females, and between males and females.

One of the unintended consequence of the world's treatment of women relates to the principle of rhythm, which states that "Everything flows, out and in. Everything has its tides. All things rise and fall. The pendulum-swing manifests in everything. The measure of the swing to the right is the measure of the swing to the left. Rhythm compensates." This means that a once male-dominated society will naturally convert to a female-dominated society as we are now experiencing, which I don't believe is healthy as a female-dominated society involves masses of women rejecting their feminine essence to embrace the masculine. On the other hand, men have been persuaded and conditioned to reject the masculine and embrace the feminine.

What I believe is natural and in the best interest of the collective is a society where, although the man stands as the head of the home, there is no domination by male or female. The man has a duty to submit to the Most High. He then leads with love, respect, humility, consideration, and kindness. Although I believe that the man should act as the head, the woman is just as powerful as she is designed, in my opinion, to be the neck that turns the head. Both men and women are indispensable, and a wise man knows that many of his blessings are stored with his woman and he must obtain the favor of the Most High in order to receive his full allotment.

Although I believe it to be wise to treat all people and things with respect, a respectful and honorable woman is to be cherished, loved, protected, and cared for. Although no one is perfect, any woman who makes a diligent effort to carry herself with respect should be held in high regard.

CHAPTER 4

VEGANISM: KARMA, COMPASSION, AND BETTER HEALTH

"Your food is supposed to be your medicine and your medicine is supposed to be your food." – African Proverb

Although I don't believe that humans, in our current form, have the level of consciousness required to describe the Highest Power by character, personality, or form, I am compelled to accept that the universe was created by something greater than myself and that the laws of the universe are transparent and can be observed and confirmed by all who wish to bear witness.

The Karmic Perspective

With that said, what if the Highest Power of the universe created angels who, after being persuaded by something other than the spirit within, came to believe that because of their superior mental and spiritual abilities that they had dominion over human beings? While believing that they had this dominion or control, and without necessity for survival, what if the angels proceeded to torture and kill humans, while ignoring their cries, because they enjoyed the way that their dead bodies smelled and tasted?

The more important question, for the sake of one's own karma and future vibrations, may be how would the humans respond? It is likely that the fears, tears, and cries of man would be seen and heard all throughout the domain of the Highest Power and mercy would be sought where none was previously given.

Currently, humans are in the position of the "angels" and animals are currently in the position of the "humans." Across the globe billions of animals are being tortured and eventually killed and man is without much mercy. However, the fifth hermetic principle, the principle of rhythm, states that "everything flows, out and in; everything has its tides; all things rise and fall; the pendulum-swing manifests in everything; the measure of the swing to the right is the measure of the swing to the left; rhythm compensates." A study of history and observation of one's personal life should provide confirmation of the validity of this principle.

The Compassionate Perspective

If we were to take a visit to a slaughterhouse and watch how animals are killed or view the same on video, those of us who seek allegiance with the Most High will hear and feel our spirits rebuke the very sight of our own eyes, which has also been the very deed of our own doing, even if indirectly through the purchase of meat, dairy, and other animal products. Many animals, after being separated from their families and forced to lived tortured, painful lives, are skinned alive, electrocuted, beaten in the head with hard objects, or cut viciously and left to bleed to death, often times while hanging upside down.

Due to our compassionate nature, many of us will feel compelled not only to stop consuming animal products but also to lend our efforts to stopping the horror that is taking place every day around the world to the billions of livestock farm animals.

Unfortunately, however, our minds, due to the domestication of our minds that has taken place through extensive conditioning, will usually have a voice that says to us "but God put the animals here for us to eat," which has allowed many to continue supporting the torture and killing of innocent animals without much of an impact on one's conscience.

But I say to those that pledge allegiance with the Most High, seek to follow your spirit and not your mind in all things for your mind has been conditioned by outside forces not in alignment with the Most High, and seek forgiveness and mercy when temptation leads you to follow the ego down the stumbling path of destruction.

Heart Disease, High Blood Pressure, Sudden Cardiac Death, & Strokes

Heart disease, which is an umbrella term referring to any disorder affecting the heart, is the number one cause of death of humans in the United States of America, Canada,

Australia, and the United Kingdom. According to the Centers for Disease Control and Prevention, heart disease accounts for approximately a quarter of all deaths in the USA, and the most common form of heart disease is coronary artery disease, which often leads to heart attack before showing any other symptom.

Animal meat is high in both cholesterol and saturated fat, which elevates blood cholesterol and causes plaque to form, which narrows and clogs the arteries that supply blood, oxygen, and nutrients to the heart, called coronary arteries, leading to a blockage of blood flow. When the heart doesn't receive enough blood, the heart muscle weakens and often leads to heart failure, which describes the state where the heart is no longer able to properly pump blood throughout the body.

Coronary artery disease also often leads to angina, a condition resulting in chest tightness or pain due to the lack of oxygen to a certain part of the heart muscle. Clogged arteries force the heart to work harder than it was designed and commonly leads to high blood pressure, stroke, and an enlarged heart, all three of which causing death on a regular basis.

Coronary artery disease also leads to an

abnormal heart rhythm, which can cause sudden cardiac death, which is the largest cause of natural death in the USA and is responsible for approximately half of all heart disease deaths. Sudden cardiac death is the loss of heart function, which is often referred to as sudden cardiac arrest. Although sudden cardiac arrest can occur during a heart attack, it differs from a heart attack as a heart attack occurs when there is a blockage of one of the arteries to the heart and the heart is not able to receive enough oxygen-rich blood. Sudden cardiac arrest occurs when the electrical system to the heart malfunctions and blood no longer flows throughout the body, including to the brain, which then results in a loss of consciousness and, if not treated immediately, death.

Another concern with clogged arteries is the blockage of blood and oxygen flow to the brain, which can lead to a stroke. According to the CDC, strokes are the fifth leading cause of death in the United States, and one American is said to die from a stroke every four minutes with approximately 800,000 people having strokes in the United States each year.

Although the human body needs cholesterol and the liver produces enough of it naturally, the danger comes when we add dietary cholesterol from food, and animal products are the only food source that contain cholesterol.

In essence, if you can't find it in your heart or mind to stop supporting the torture and killing of innocent animals, your heart and brain are being setup for physical failure. There are no coincidences in the universe, and the laws and ways of the universe should be sought after and aligned with to the best of one's ability. Prayer, several times a day to the Most High, should be used as a supplement to increase one's capacity to obtain righteousness in both thought and in deed.

Cancer

Cancer is the second leading cause of death in the USA right behind heart disease. Dioxins, which are a group of chemical compounds, are highly toxic and cancerous, and the US Environmental Protection Agency states that more than 90% of human exposure to dioxin comes from food, mainly animal products. Dioxins settle and accumulate in fat and, therefore, the more animal products that we eat, the more dioxins we accumulate and store.

LaFoy Orlando Thomas III, Esq.

According to the National Cancer Institute, cooking meat at high temperatures, such as grilling, broiling, and frying creates cancer-causing compounds called heterocyclic amines and polycyclic aromatic hydrocarbons, which are mutagenic as they cause changes in DNA.

Also, in a study by the University of California at San Diego, a sugar molecule named Neu5Gc, which is naturally found in non-human mammals, has been shown to cause cancer in mice, who similar to humans do not naturally grow Neu5Gc, and beef, pork, and lamb are rich in Neu5Gc. Being foreign to the human body, our immune systems likely produce antibodies against Neu5Gc, which causes inflammation, and chronic inflammation is commonly known to promote tumor formation.

Vegan Food Options

Today there is a plethora of food options that leave the practice of slaughtering animals simply unnecessary and cruel. Many grocery stores have natural or health food sections that, combined with fresh fruits and vegetables, make living the vegan lifestyle convenient, enjoyable, and comforting. Although I eat certain vegan foods, such as broccoli and cauliflower, that are not approved by Dr. Sebi, he is a great resource to research to learn how to eat and heal yourself.

To start the day, there are various brands of vegan breakfast cereals that work perfectly with almond milk, coconut milk, or cashew milk. Vegan waffles, pancakes, granola, oatmeal cooked with almond milk and topped with fruit or cashew milk ice cream, breakfast potatoes, and smoothies with added spirulina or flax seeds are additional breakfast items to enjoy.

For lunch and dinner, lentils, whole grain pasta, brown rice noodles, brown rice, quinoa, black beans, pinto beans, kidney beans, kale greens, collard greens, spinach, onions, sweet potatoes, corn, broccoli, cauliflower, potatoes, tomatoes, and mushrooms are some key staples that are both filling and delicious when seasoned and prepared to taste. Avocado is a great tasting and healthy cheese replacement and can be used in many meals. It is important to note that when combining legumes like beans, lentils, or peanut butter with grains like brown rice or wheat bread, a complete protein is had, which means the meal contains all nine of the essential amino acids.

Early in the vegan transition, careful

attention should be paid to the amount of protein, iron, and fiber consumed. It's a good habit to try to add as many different colors of fruits and vegetables to each meal as possible to prevent any key vitamin deficiencies that both vegans and meat eaters often suffer from.

Veganism as a Gateway to Spiritual Enlightenment

After following the counsel of your spirit and going vegan, as is also the case with obeying your spirit regarding other endeavors, you become gifted with knowledge of many of the secrets and keys to the universe. One such secret is the amazing benefit of the sun.

Sun light, especially absorbed through the eyes while sun gazing, is the best natural supply for vitamin D, and it also is a key contributor to maintaining a positive attitude and an insightful mind. Sun light activates the pineal gland, which is often referred to as our third eye or spiritual eye. The pineal gland secretes melanin, which is a biochemical substance that regulates all bodily functions and glands. Black people have the highest level of melanin of all of the races as evidenced by our typically darker skin, hair, and eye colors.

As a part of its duty of regulating all bodily functions, melanin attaches to synthetic chemicals, such as drugs and food additives, in the body and attempts to either neutralize them or escort them out of the body. This is a major key to maintaining good health, but when the body is overloaded with harmful chemicals, the combination of melanin and the harmful substance remain lodged together in the body and damages everything with a high concentration of melanin, including the brain and sexual organs. For this reason, Black people assume a higher level of risk to their brains and bodies after consuming illegal and legal drugs, alcohol, tobacco, and processed foods.

The pineal gland requires sunlight to secrete melanin and is shaped like a pine cone. A lack of sunlight often leads to mild depression or melancholy due to the lack of melanin secretion by the pineal gland. The pineal gland is located in the middle of our brains.

As a side note, tap water is filled with fluoride, which calcifies the pineal gland and converts super humans into simple, ordinary beings, who are often unable to think clearly, work in harmony, or empathize with others due to their inadequate melanin levels. Therefore, I strongly recommend the avoidance of tap water and the purchase and consumption of spring water only.

I also strongly recommend avoiding all genetically modified organisms (GMO). Foods that are genetically modified have had their genetic makeup, or DNA, modified. Although there are many things written about GMO products, I will only speak from personal experience. After abstaining from GMO products for a period of time, consuming GMO products causes my body and mind to show signs of rejection, and I believe that we should listen to our bodies when deciding what we should and should not consume. My signs of rejection have included headaches, stomachaches, and a lack of mental clarity.

In the United States, it has been estimated that over 90% of all potatoes, soy, and corn are genetically modified with the main exception being for organic products. Organic potatoes and corn are okay to eat and even recommended. However, especially for men, I recommend avoiding even organic soy products as they promote emotional instability due to its estrogen altering properties. I've had experiences where I would feel unreasonably emotional about certain events that in my mind I knew I was indifferent about. After eliminating soy from my diet these types of experiences no longer occurred. It is important to note that many processed foods, including processed vegan foods, contain soy.

After Going Vegan

In addition to feeling better about yourself as you would no longer be supporting the torture and killing of innocent animals with your daily diet, your mind and body respond immediately to your dietary adjustment after going vegan.

One of the greatest benefits for men is an improved sexual drive and the ability to perform for extended and, in some cases, infinite lengths of time. For women, pain from menstrual cramps disappears or reduces significantly. With the removal of meat and dairy from the diet, energy is increased, the skin clears, and extra body weight is immediately lost in many cases. Will power is also increased, which can be used to aid in the attainment of any worthy goal.

The mind also clears after abstaining from meat and dairy and the ability to properly rationalize, empathize, and think of new ventures emerges. Your life path shall become easier to identify and an immediate change for the better in your personal vibration and relationship with the universe becomes apparent.

Transitioning to a vegan diet is as much of a spiritual journey as it is physical and your relationship with the Most High shall likely show improvement and become a focal point, which I believe is reason enough to immediately start the transition.

Trap Vegan Clothing Brand

If you are vegan or in the process of transitioning, please support my clothing brand Trap Vegan by visiting TrapVeganBrand.com. The brand represents spirit, compassion, and the hustle. Spirit represents our internal compass, compassion is for both humans and animals, and the hustle represents building wealth via investing, purpose alignment, and entrepreneurship. Represent and use your fashion to start a life-saving conversation.

CHAPTER 5

NUMEROLOGY: THE SPIRITUAL ESSENCE OF NUMBERS

"The kingdom of heaven is within you; and whoever shall know himself shall find it." – Egyptian Proverb

The mysteries of self, the Earth, and the planets of this universe are many, and certain sects of society have discouraged many of the Earth's inhabitants from seeking such knowledge. Without true knowledge of self and the universe, one is unable to fully understand and face the necessary challenges leading to self-improvement and self-mastery, both of which are required to obtain spiritual mastery and to identify and carry out one's true life purpose. The Most High has allowed to be made available to us knowledge pertaining to our truest personality and character traits, along with information pertaining to past life karma, which often rings true to one's current life if mastery of such character deficiencies is not obtained.

The Power of Numbers and Living in the Flow

The Most High definitely deals in numbers. That is my first conclusion after indulging in the study of numerology, or the science of number energies. In addition to being extremely accurate, numerology appears to also have a highly predictive quality, which can allow one to gracefully live in the flow of the universe. From gaining insights into the natural path that your life should take to knowing the energy of each year, month, or day based on your personal biorhythm, numerology is a science, although metaphysical, that deserves both respect and keen observation.

Each number carries with it its own unique energy vibration. Becoming aware of the numbers that represent your core being and the days of your life is of the utmost importance if one wishes to live in harmony with one's divine purpose. Throughout this chapter, you will be exposed to how the numbers of your life provide insights into things ranging from the gifts that have been granted to you for the purpose of carrying out your destiny to what you can expect to achieve or be challenged to overcome during each cycle of your lifetime.

The General Energy of Numbers

Numbers have both positive and negative aspects. Being in tune or not with one's spirit dictates, to a large degree, which aspect of any particular number will represent you at any given moment. The ego prefers to entice us to carry the lower vibrations of our numbers while the spirit wishes to shine brightly and allow the most appreciative, praiseworthy components of ourselves to be on display.

The number 1 is connected to the masculine principle and, at its best, represents ambition, leadership, independence, innovation, confidence, and creativity. At its lower vibration, the 1 may be egotistical, in lack of self-esteem, and show a disregard for, or a weakened relationship with, one's higher self or spirt within and, instead of seeking alignment with the Most High, the 1 may instead focus its energy on gaining the approval of other human beings and is typically very sensitive to criticism.

The number 2 is connected to the feminine principle and, at its best, represents unity, harmony, consideration, cooperation, patience, sensitivity, and a keen attention to details. At its lower vibration, the 2 can be possessive, jealous, indecisive, and overly passive.

The number 3, at its best, represents joy, creativity, optimism, and a gift for self-expression. At its lower vibration, the 3 may display a sharp, wounding tongue, selfishness, and engage in the act of spreading negative words which carry negative vibrations concerning others.

The number 4, at its best, represents honesty, integrity, practicality, discipline, hard work, building, security, and stability. At its lower vibration, the 4 tends to represent rigidity, a lack of discipline, and also a need to be controlling.

The number 5, at its best, represents magnetism, energy, enthusiasm, intellectual curiosity, youthfulness, freedom, change, and a need to travel. At its lower vibration, the 5 may demonstrate an inability to control physical desires, an inability to focus, and a misuse of freedom.

The number 6, at its best, represents love, family, loyalty, nurturing, counseling, teaching, and balance. At its lower vibration, the 6 represents a lack of balance, self-neglect, can be unforgiving, and may even be too idealistic, nosy, or interfering.

The number 7 is very spiritual and, at its best, represents inner wisdom, intuition, intellect, and strong analyzation capabilities. At its lower vibration, the 7 can represent the mindset of a perfectionist and can be very introverted, displaying isolation issues, which can make it hard to create and maintain friendships.

The number 8, at its best, represents self-mastery, wealth, business success, and accomplishment. At its lower vibration, the 8 can become intimidating and too engrossed in the mission of making money and may prioritize profit over family and the spiritual laws of the universe, which typically is demonstrated by a misuse of power and authority.

The number 9 is also very spiritual and, at its best, represents wisdom, intuition, genuine compassion, service, and an ability to overcome setbacks. At its lower vibration, the 9 may be shy, intolerant, selfish, greedy, and vulnerable to health issues. The number 9 is also the number of endings, which can be positive or negative.

The number 10 is a karmic number, which relates to lessons that need to be learned during this lifetime in order for our souls to evolve. Unlike the other karmic numbers of 13, 14, 16, and 19, 10 is not a karmic debt number but instead represents a fulfilment of past karmic debt.

The number 11, similar to 22 and 33, is a master number and represents a higher calling during this lifetime. The higher calling of the 11 is that of the spiritual messenger and inspirational leader with the ability to raise the level of consciousness of the world. The 11 is highly intuitive, possibly more so than all of the other numbers. At its lower vibration, the 11 will operate based on the vibrations of the 2 as 11 is reduced to 2 (1+1=2).

The karmic debt number 13 represents a previous misuse of wittiness or self-expression and likely hurt others with creative means of expression.

The karmic debt number 14 represents a past misuse of freedom and a neglect of hard work or responsibility, possibly both.

The karmic debt number 16 represents an abuse of love or family in a past life and family or friends may have been taken for granted.

The karmic debt number 19 represents a misuse of wisdom or spiritual gifts, such as that of a misleading, selfish, or greedy religious preacher.

The number 22 represents the master builder, which includes extraordinary vision, strong ambition, wisdom, intuition, and the ability to build things for the greater good of the world. At its lower vibration, the 22 will operate on the vibrations of the 4 as 22 is reduced to 4 (2+2=4).

The number 33 represents the highest degree of love and compassion for the world and often displays itself through service for others. The 33, at its lower vibration, will operate at the level of the 6 as 33 is reduced to 6 (3+3=6).

Life Path Numbers

A person's life path number represents the innate gifts that a person has been blessed with in order to assist the person in fulfilling the person's destiny during this lifetime. Considered one of the most important numbers in numerology, the life path number can reveal the best areas of study and occupation based on one's natural abilities and interests.

The life path number is calculated by reducing and then adding up the numbers associated with your date of birth and then reducing the final number if it isn't already a single digit. For example, if a person's birthday is December 11, 1990, the math would be done as follows: December reduces to 3 as the 12th month is reduced by adding the 1 and the 2. 11 is a master number, and it isn't reduced when it's the final number. In this case, 11 isn't a final number so 11 reduces to 2 as 1+1=2. 1990 reduces to 1 as 1+9+9+0=19, which is further reduced to 1 as 1+9=10, which is reduced to 1.

To find the life path number, you add the 3 from December plus the 2 from the 11th, and finally the 1 from 1990 to get a total of 6. Or, to keep things simple, you can Google your birthdate along with the words "life path" to discover your life path number.

A person with a birthdate of December 11, 1990 has the life path number of 6, which makes the person perfect for counseling, teaching, nurturing, and raising a family. The 6 is the number of love and service. Michael Jackson, whose birthdate was August 29, 1958, had a 6 life path number, symbolizing his compassionate, healing, and nurturing nature.

It is important to note that if your final calculation results in 11 or 22 you do not reduce further. Instead, you embrace the fact that you have a master life path number and also the fact that much will be required of you.

A person with a 1 life path number is meant to develop their innate talents relating to leadership and independence, so entrepreneurship and executive positions work best for this life path number. Dr. Martin Luther King Jr., whose birthdate was January 15, 1929, had a 1 life path number, which made him a great candidate to lead the civil rights movement.

A person with a 2 life path number should excel in fields that require sensitivity, compassion, attention to detail, and the ability to be cooperative or a team player. The peace seeking and compassionate former American president Barack Obama, whose birthdate was August 4, 1961, has a 2 life path number.

A person with a 3 life path number has the natural gifts of being creative and also the ability to express one's self with much articulation. Effective communication is not much of a challenge for the life path 3. The highly creative and articulate American comedian Chris Rock, whose birthdate was February 7, 1965, has a 3 life path number.

The life path of 4 will bless one with the ability to work hard and build things, such as businesses or efficient systems. Bill Gates, whose birthdate was October 28, 1955, has a 4 life path number.

A person with a 5 life path number embraces freedom, change and travel, so careers where one can change the people and places that the person sees each day are encouraged. The top careers for this person may be in entrepreneurship or sales and marketing. Civil rights activists Malcom X, whose birthdate was May 19, 1925, had a 5 life path number, which was demonstrated through his "any means necessary" approach to gaining freedom.

A person with a 7 life path number is likely to be very spiritual and also great in areas where one can study and master subjects, which can range from computer science to the laws of the universe. American boxing legend and spiritual teacher Muhammad Ali, whose birthdate was January 17, 1942, had a 7 life path number, which should be no surprise given his heightened level of spiritual awareness. I, myself, am a life path 7 as well.

A person with an 8 life path number is a natural leader and will likely experience a stage of self-mastery. Entrepreneurship or executive positions are best suited for the 8's natural gifts. South African revolutionary, politician, and philanthropist Nelson Rolihlahla Mandela, whose birthdate was July 18, 1918, had an 8 life path number.

A person with a 9 life path number has the innate ability to connect and care for others. People with 9 life path numbers may make great teachers, counselors, and social workers. Bob Marley, whose birthdate was February 6, 1945, Mahatma Gandhi, who birthdate was October 2, 1869, and Mother Teresa, whose birthdate was August 26, 1910, were all members of the life path number 9 family.

The 11 life path number is the path of the spiritual messenger and inspirational leader. Careers that allow one to inspire and enlighten others work best for the 11 life path number. Civil rights activist Rosa Parks, whose birthdate was February 4, 1913, had an 11 life path number. She was definitely inspirational to say the least.

The 22 life path number represents the master builder and ideal career choices would include political leadership positions and businesses that impact the world for the better. American musician, poet, actor, and political activist Tupac Shakur, whose birthdate was June 16, 1971, had the master 22 life path number. No wonder he was considered one of the hardest working people in the entertainment business. Also, at his best and highest vibration, his messages were able to touch and inspire millions, if not billions, of people all over the world.

Destiny Numbers

Although a divine power may ultimately determine one's name, a person's name determines, or at least reveals, the person's destiny. Working in conjunction with the life path number, the destiny numbers provide insight into the highest purpose of a person during this lifetime and the path of least resistance to success. Using the full name as it appears on the birth certificate, adding the numbers associated with the letters from a person's first, middle, and last names reveals the general destiny or mission of the person. Although married names, adopted names, and nicknames have their influences on the vibrational makeup of a person, the name found on the birth certificate carries the most significance.

Each letter in each name is represented by a number and carries a vibration. The letters A, J, and S are represented by the number 1. B, K, and T are represented by the number 2. C, L, and U are represented by the number 3. D, M, and V are represented by the number 4. E, N, and W are represented by the number 5. F, O, and X are represented by the number 6. G, P, and Y are represented by the number 7. H, Q, and Z are represented by the number 8. I and R are represented by the number 9.

If any number shows up more than 2 or 3 times in a person's full name, it is highly likely that the associated traits are easily identifiable in said person. Also, the reduced sum of a person's first, middle, or last name will reveal key characteristics of a person. The reduced sum of a person's middle name, for example, reveals talents and personality traits that the person may try to hide early in life.

To illustrate how the calculations of each name and then the destiny number is done, let's use the name of South African leader Nelson Rolihlahla Mandela. The first name Nelson consists of the numbers 5, 5, 3, 1, 6, and 5. The sum of the numbers from his first name is 25, which is reduced to 7, indicating a spiritual and wise nature. Also, worthy of observation is the amount of 5s, representing freedom and change, in his first name: three!

The middle name Rolihlahla consists of the numbers 9, 6, 3, 9, 8, 3, 1, 8, 3, and 1 for a total of 51, which is reduced to 6, representing his loving and compassionate nature. In his middle name, the humanitarian 9 appears two times, the loving, serving 6 appears once, the creative and highly expressive 3 appears three times, the leading and ambitious 8 appears twice, and the leading and ambitious 1 appears twice.

The last name of Mandela consists of the numbers 4, 1, 5, 4, 5, 3, and 1 for a total of 23, which is reduced to 5, representing freedom and change, which was a common theme from the large number of 5s in his first name.

To calculate his destiny number, you add the 7 from his first name to the 6 from his middle name and then the 5 from his last name for a total of 18, which is reduced to 9. His destiny number is 9, which is the number of the humanitarian. Considering this, along with his 8 life path number and his large number of 5s in his name profile, it is revealed that Nelson Mandela was destined to be a humanitarian leader fighting for freedom and change. This is the power of numerology! It is important to note that hyphenated last names count as one single name, which is also the case for compound last names. However, a person with multiple middle names would compute each middle name separately.

A person with a 1 destiny number is destined to develop into a leader and embrace a high level of independence.

A person with a 2 destiny number is destined to become a person with the ability to create peace and harmony between others and to also be a cooperative team player.

A person with a 3 destiny number is destined to be a creative and share his or her optimism to inspire others.

A person with a destiny number 4 is destined to work hard and build something, such as a business, a large collection of real estate, or intellectual property.

A person with a 5 destiny number is destined to be a free spirt, have the ability to adapt to change, and to be very resourceful.

A person with a 6 destiny number is destined to serve in some capacity and to be very caring and nurturing.

A person with a 7 destiny number is destined to live a life seeking truths, much of which from meditation and going within, and to then share his or her collection of wisdom with the world. I, the author of this book, am both a life path 7 and a destiny 7; hence, the creation and publication of this book.

A person with an 8 destiny number is destined to be a leader and a master of self. The 8 has the task of achieving in business or socially and to stay conscious of the greater good of the world and of the power of karma by never disregarding the laws of the universe.

A person with a 9 destiny number is destined to be a humanitarian and to become a master of unconditional love.

A person with a master number 11 destiny number is destined to be an inspirational leader and spiritual messenger.

A person with a master number 22 destiny number is destined to use spiritual wisdom to build something to benefit the world as a whole. Although my destiny number is 7, my last name equals 22, which shall contribute to the success of this book.

A person with a 33 master destiny number is destined to enlighten the world regarding the power of love in its purest form. Forgiving, unconditional, and relentless, love's brightest attributes are revealed to the world by the destiny number 33 being.

Soul Numbers

The soul number represents a person's

truest desires at his or her core and often is the motivation or driving force for a person's actions and intentions. The soul number is determined by calculating the vowels in a person's name. Vowels are the letters a, e, i, o, u, and y when y is the only vowel sound, meaning it's not silent or unpronounced, in the syllable. For example, the y in the month of May isn't a vowel since the letter a is the pronounced vowel and the y is unpronounced. In the name Toby, the y is a vowel since it is pronounced. Y is also a vowel when it combines with another vowel in the same syllable to create a diphthong. A diphthong is created when a syllable starts with the sound of one vowel and then transitions to the sound of the other vowel, such as in the word "boy."

Nelson Rolihlahla Mandela has the vowel numbers in his first name of 5 and 6, which equals 11, which is reduced to 2. The middle name has the vowel numbers of 6, 9, 1, and 1, which totals 17, which is reduced to 8. The last name has the vowel numbers of 1, 5, and 1, which totals 7. Adding the 2 from the first name to the 8 from the middle name and then the 7 from the last name equals 17, which is reduced to 8. Another revelation that Nelson Mandela had a true, burning desire to lead his people to freedom and to dismantle the apartheid system of South Africa. He was born to be a leader and had a desire to fulfil his destiny.

A person with a 1 soul number wishes for independence and leadership. A person with a 2 soul number wants peace, harmony, and to be supportive above all else. A person with a 3 soul number wishes to uplift others and to express his or her creativity. A person with a 4 soul number desires to create and execute a plan and to build something of lasting value, such as generational wealth.

A person with a 5 soul number desires to network, travel, and be free physically and sexually. A person with a 6 soul number wishes to love, serve, nurture, and may desire to have as many children as possible. A person with a 7 soul number desires solitude, time to study, and often wishes to learn about self and the mysteries of the universe. A person with an 8 soul number desires positions of leadership, as mentioned above with Nelson Mandela. A person with a 9 soul number is highly compassionate and often desires for all living beings to be treated with consideration, love, and respect.

A person with a master 11 soul number often wants to be in a position of leadership since he or she is influenced by the two number 1s that make up 11. Also, the 11 soul number often wants to enlighten the world as a whole or at least the person's world around him or her. People with the master 22 soul number wish to build something for the greater good of the world. A person with the master 33 soul number desires to spread love to all and to treat love as an infinite resource.

Personality Numbers

The personality number reveals how other see you, even if you don't see yourself in the same light. The personality number represents the outer you and is calculated by adding together the consonants of your full name. The consonants are all of the letters that aren't vowels. Using the great Nelson Mandela as another example, the consonants in his first name are 5, 3, 1, and 5, which totals 14, which is reduced to 5. The consonants in his middle name are 9, 3, 8, 3, 8, and 3, which totals 34, which is reduced to 7. The consonants in his last name are 4, 5, 4, and 3, which add up to 16, which is reduced to 7. Adding the 5 from his first name with the 7 from his middle name and then the 7 from his last name, the total equals 19, which is reduced to 1, revealing that others viewed him as confident, courageous, and as someone who was truly worthy of leadership.

A person with a 2 personality number likely comes off as peaceful, cooperative, and shy. A person with a 3 personality number comes off as friendly, charming, creative, and optimistic. A person with a 4 personality number comes off as honest, reliable, and hard working. A person with a 5 personality number comes off as attractive, free-spirited, and sensual. A person with a 6 personality number comes off as a great counselor and also as very nurturing.

A person with a 7 personality number comes off as mysterious, intelligent, and introverted. A person with an 8 personality number comes off as ambitious, strong, intelligent, and as having a high business acumen. A person with a 9 personality number comes off as wise, tolerant, compassionate, and generous. A person with a master 11 personality number comes off as inspirational, intelligent, and highly spiritual. A person with a master 22 personality number comes off as hard working, determined, responsible, honest, and as a masterful builder.

Maturity Numbers

The maturity number represents the person who gradually appears as one evolves and finds his or her true self. The influence or impact of the energy from the maturity number is believed to come into effect around the age of 35 and can be fully felt by the age of 50. The maturity number, which is very easy to calculate, is found by adding together the life path number and the destiny number and then reducing to a single digit unless, of course, the final number is a master number. Using Nelson Mandela as yet another example, adding his life path number of 8 to his destiny number of 9 totals 17, which is reduced to 8, revealing his true self was a leader and a person of accomplishment.

A person with a 1 maturity number can expect to grow into a leader and gain a higher need for independence. A person with a 2 maturity number will develop the ability to be a peacemaker and learn to negotiate, compromise, and be cooperative. A person with a 3 maturity number shall develop and embrace the natural abilities of positive thinking, expression, and creativity. A person with a 4 maturity number will learn the importance of hard work and during the maturity years a person with a 4 maturity number can be expected to turn dreams into reality. A person with a 5 maturity number will likely maintain a youthful spirit and will often seek change, excitement, travel, and freedom. A person with a 5 maturity number will also likely be highly attractive to the opposite sex.

A person with a 6 maturity number, the number of love and service, will likely grow into the role of the humanitarian and is also likely to be highly family oriented. A person with a 7 maturity number will realize his or her essence as a seeker of truth and the need for solitude, silence, and wisdom attainment. A person with an 8 maturity number will likely grow into an accomplished person, a leader, and also reach the pinnacle of self-mastery if the spiritual principles of the universe are honored. A person with a 9 maturity number is a loving, compassionate humanitarian.

A person with a master 11 maturity number will likely gain an appreciation for all things spiritual and also grow into the ability to uplift and inspire others. A person with master 22 maturity number will grow into the master builder role and will likely be grounded in practicality. A person with a master 33 maturity number can expect to master the art of loving both thyself and others in a balanced, responsible manner. A person with a 33 maturity number can expect to be of great service to the world, using love as the tool of all tools.

Major Cycles: Formative, Productive, and Harvest

A person's life is divided into three major cycles consisting of approximately 28 years each. The first, which is determined by the month of birth, is the formative period. For example, a person whose month of birth is during the month of February will have the formative period of his or her life guided by the lessons of the 2: cooperation, teamwork, peacemaking, and attention to details. Someone whose month of birth is during the month of June, for example, will have the first cycle themed around nurturing, service, and learning to be balanced.

The second major cycle, based on the day of the month that a person was born, is the productive period of a person's life. For example, if a person was born on the 4th day of any month, the second major cycle will be based on the theme of the 4: responsibility, hard work, structure, integrity, and building. If a person was born on the 11th, which is a master number, the second cycle will be based on the calling of the spiritual messenger. If rejected, the 11 calling may be reduced to the themes of the 2, which may lead one to positions involving peacemaking, negotiating, and teamwork.

The day of birth is also considered the birthday number and reveals natural gifts held by the person. For example, entertainers Jay-Z (Shawn Carter) and his wife Beyoncé Knowles both have 4 birthday numbers, which reveals their natural ability to work hard and to build things of lasting value, which both have done. It also reveals that both have likely by now learned the importance of having integrity and both are likely strong believers in karma.

The third major cycle, determined by the year of birth, is the harvest period and reveals how one is likely to spend the later years of life. For example, a person born in 1990, which is reduced to the number 1 (1+9+9+0=19, which is reduced to 10, which is reduced to 1), will likely have independence and confidence during the later years of life and may even hold a position of leadership. A person born in 1983 (1+9+8+3=21, which is reduced to 3 as 2+1=3) will have a harvest period centered in the themes of the 3: fun, friends, optimism, creativity, and self-expression. Of course, learning the lessons of the prior cycles and generating positive karma will have an impact on the quality of any cycle or day of a person's life.

Personal Year Numbers

Although the major cycle number is the most impactful influence in carrying out your destiny, each year, based on a nine-year cycle, has its own theme for a person's life based on his or her own personal biorhythm. After the influence of the major cycle and personal year, a person also has personal months and days that have their own influence and must be honored in order to keep one on the path of least resistance and in sync with the universe.

In order to calculate a person's personal year, which starts in January, one must first calculate the universal year. For example, the year 2018 was a 2 universal year (2+0+1+8=11, which is reduced to 2 as 1+1=2). A universal 2 year brings the energies of harmony, peace, and cooperation. It is a year of slow, patient development. 2019 is a 3 universal year.

After calculating the current universal year, add the reduced digit from the month of birth and the reduced digit from the day of birth. For example, in 2018, a person with a birthday of April 6 will calculate by adding the universal year of 2 with the 4 from April and the 6 from the 6th for a total of 12, which is reduced to 3. A person in a personal 3 year should expect to have fun and to not work too hard. A 3 personal year is great for creativity and self-expression.

A 1 personal year is good for starting new businesses, new relationships, and new projects. A 2 personal year is good for cooperation, teamwork, and patience. A personal 4 year is a good time for building, starting new businesses, and working really hard to secure the future. A personal 5 year is good for traveling, making changes, and taking risks. A 6 personal year is good for nurturing others and being attentive to family matters. A personal 7 year is good for studying, focusing within, rest, meditation, and lots of prayer. A personal 8 year is good for handling business, embracing leadership opportunities, and one can expect to be recognized and rewarded for business efforts and hard work. A 9 personal year is a time for harvest, letting go, and completing projects started in prior years.

Personal Month Numbers

Personal months are calculated by adding the number of the personal year to the number of the calendar month. For example, a person in a 3 personal year will be in a 4 personal month in January as you would add the 3 from the personal year to the 1 from the calendar month of January. That same person would be in a 6 personal month in December as you would add the 3 from the personal year to the 3 from the calendar month as December is reduced as 1+2=3. In a personal 6 month one can expect to have more than normal family demands, which is also the case in a personal 6 year.

Personal months are a great time to catch up or focus on things that were missed or neglected during the personal year that represented the same number. For example, in a 3 month in a 4 year you can take the opportunity to focus on having fun even though the theme of the 4 year is related to hard work. The energy of the year is the stronger of the two, but taking advantage of the energy of the personal month is highly recommended.

Personal Day Numbers

The personal day number is calculated by adding the number from the calendar day to the number of your personal month. For example, a person in a 4 personal month would have a 5 personal day on the 1st of the month. That same person would have a 9 personal day on the 23rd of the month as you would add the 4 from the personal month to the 5 from the calendar day of the month as 23 is reduced to 5 (2+3=5). The energies, although much less subtle, are similar to the corresponding numbers from personal years and personal months.

Pinnacle Numbers

Similar to our major cycles, we also have four pinnacle numbers that reveal the areas in our lives, at particular times, which we are mostly likely to excel and reach our highest achievements.

Our first pinnacle covers our first 27-35 years of existence, depending on our particular life path number. The length of a person's first pinnacle number is calculated by subtracting the person's life path number from 36. For example, a person with a 4 life path number will have a first pinnacle period covering the ages of birth to 32. A person with a master life path number will use the reduced single digit number when subtracting the life path number from 36. For example, a person with a master 22 life path number would have a first pinnacle cover the ages of birth until 32 as 36-4=32 and since 22 is reduced to 4.

The length of the second pinnacle period is calculated by adding nine years to the end of the first pinnacle. For example, a person with a 4 life path number will have a second pinnacle cycle covering ages 32 to 41. The length of the third pinnacle is calculated the same as the second pinnacle by adding nine years to the end of the second pinnacle. So a person with a 4 life path number will experience a third pinnacle period covering the ages of 41 to 50. The fourth pinnacle cycle, which is potentially the longest, covers the end of the third pinnacle until death.

To find your first pinnacle number, add the month of your birth to your reduced day of birth. For example, a person born on February 8th will have a 1 first pinnacle number as 2+8=10, which is reduced to 1. When a 1 shows up as the first or second pinnacle, the opportunities to develop independence and leadership qualities are likely to be encountered. When the third or fourth pinnacle is a 1 there will be great opportunities to succeed later in life in leadership roles. Pinnacle numbers that appear in the first and second period are likely related to the opportunity to develop such talents and third and fourth pinnacle numbers typically apply to the use, recognition, and benefit of related gifts and attributes.

To find your second pinnacle number, add the day of birth to the reduced year of birth. For example, a person born on the 11th of any month during the year of 1985 will have a second pinnacle of 7 as 11 is reduced to 2 and 1985 is reduced to 5 (2+5=7). A person with a 7 pinnacle number will find the path of least resistance to involve pursuits in spirituality or areas of scientific specialization.

To calculate a person's third pinnacle number, add the first pinnacle number to the second pinnacle number. For example, a person with a 1 first pinnacle number and a 7 second pinnacle number will have an 8 third pinnacle number. People with 8 pinnacle numbers either have the opportunity to develop business acumen and personal power during the first two pinnacles or demonstrate and benefit from said mastery during the third and fourth pinnacles.

The fourth pinnacle number is calculated by adding the month of birth to the reduced year of birth. For example, a person born in February of 1985 will have a fourth pinnacle number of 7 as February is represented by 2 and 1985 is reduced to 5.

It is important to know that when calculating the pinnacle number to reduce any master or karmic debt numbers in the calculating process but not if the final digit is a master number.

A person with a 2 pinnacle number will be presented with the opportunity to develop cooperative, harmonious relationships if the pinnacle is the first or the second and a chance to use such abilities to your greatest benefit if the 2 pinnacle number is either the third or fourth pinnacle number.

A person with a 3 pinnacle number will be afforded the opportunity to develop skills of self-expression and creativity during the early pinnacles and the ability to profit from such skills if the 3 pinnacle is one of the latter two pinnacles.

A person with a 4 pinnacle number will learn to work hard, have structure, and build for the future if the 4 pinnacle number is one of the early pinnacle numbers and the ability to profit from such attributes if the 4 pinnacle appears during the latter two pinnacle periods.

A person with a 5 pinnacle number can expect change, traveling, and opportunities for sales and promotion. If the 5 pinnacle number appears early then the person will be given opportunities to learn to adjust to change and a person with a 5 pinnacle number in the latter two pinnacles will have the opportunity to thrive from the adaptability to change.

A person with a 6 pinnacle number will either learn to devote the appropriate level of love and responsibility to family or thrive in family relationships because of the ability to apply a balanced level of love and commitment to both family and outsiders. In the latter two cycles, a person with a 6 pinnacle number will thrive in teaching, counseling, and other nurturing roles.

A person with a 9 pinnacle number will learn the importance of expressing universal love and compassion for everyone in the early pinnacles and will likely find an opportunity to benefit greatly from such abilities if the 9 appears in the latter two cycles.

A person with a master 11 pinnacle number will likely experience tremendous spiritual growth if the 11 appears as one of the first two cycles and the ability to be a benefit to self and the world if the 11 appears during one of the latter two cycles.

A person with a master 22 pinnacle number will have the ability to build, structure, and organize something of tremendous value for the world.

Challenge Numbers

Whereas our pinnacle numbers make us aware of our greatest possibilities of achievement, our challenge numbers, on the other hand, point to the potential areas of difficulty that we are likely to encounter and that are required on our individual paths of evolvement.

A person's challenge numbers cover the same period of time as the pinnacle numbers, so a person's first pinnacle number and first challenge number run concurrently. To calculate the first challenge number, subtract the month of birth from the day of birth. For example, a person born on February 3rd will have a first challenge number of 1 as you would subtract the 2 for February from the 3 for the day of birth. A person with a 1 challenge number will likely face circumstances that prepare the person for leadership and independence.

A person's second challenge number is calculated by subtracting the day of birth from the year of birth, so a person born on the 11th of any month and in the year of 1983 will have a 1 second challenge number as 11 reduces to 2 and 1983 reduces to 3. 3-2=1, but even if the year was 2 and the day was 3 the challenge number would still be 1 as negatives convert to positives.

A person's third challenge number is calculated by subtracting the first challenge number from the second challenge number, so if a person has a 1 first challenge number and a 1 for second challenge number the third challenge number would be 0 as 1-1=0. A person with a 0 for a challenge number has the opportunity to create the life of his or her choice and to help make the world a better place, but good choices will be required throughout the pinnacle period and one can expect several forks in the road.

A person's fourth challenge number is calculated by subtracting the month of birth from the year of birth, so a person born in August of 1984 will have a fourth challenge number of 4 as August represents 8 and 1984 reduces to 4, and 4-8=-4, which converts to a positive 4. A person with a 4 for a challenge number has to learn the value of hard work, discipline, and practicality.

A person with a number 2 challenge number will have to learn to be sensitive to others, balanced, and also learn to have harmonious relationships. A person with a 3 challenge number will have to learn the art of self-expression and using creative energy positively.

A person with a 5 challenge number will likely have to evolve into a space where one can use freedom responsibly and not abusively. Learning to deal with change can also be in the cards. A person with a 6 challenge number will learn to be of service to others and also learn the value of responsibility and taking care of family. A person with a 7 challenge number will likely have to overcome the desire to be isolated and also learn to acknowledge the voice of the spirit within.

A person with an 8 challenge number will likely have to learn the proper place of universal law and its connectedness to lasting power and wealth accumulation.

Miscellaneous Numbers

There are many other numbers that have a vibrational influence on our lives, including our house or apartment numbers, the street numbers that we live and work on, and even the reduced number of our car license plates. For example, a house with an address starting with house number 5566 will likely have the energy of the master number 22 and 4 as 5+5+6+6=22.

This will be a home of hard work and building for the future, possibly even building something that will have a lasting impact on the world if the occupant is living at his or her highest vibration.

The home should also have the energy of the 5 and the 6 as the individual numbers that create the reduced sum are also considered in just about all numerology profiles. Although a home with a 5566 home number will be a place of hard work, it is also likely to be a place that requires freedom and change, which represent the 5 energy, and balance, nurturing, and service, which represent the 6. The numbers are quite revealing! Take a look and see for yourself…

CHAPTER 6

CREATING GENERATIONAL WEALTH

"Gold labors diligently and contentedly for the wise owner who finds for it profitable employment, multiplying even as the flocks of the field." – The Richest Man in Babylon

The Need for Financial Literacy

In addition to our need to develop spiritually as a collective, one of the most important and urgent conditions faced by many members of society is the lack of financial literacy. Many members of society are without an inclination of even a reasonable method by which one can accumulate generational wealth and secure it for the utilization of future generations.

The purpose of this book is to enlighten and bring awareness to the power of alignment: alignment with the Most High, alignment with the universe, and alignment with natural law. However, I also understand that spirituality and alignment are more likely to be a consistent focus when the mindset of scarcity has been abandoned and the person can no longer envision a future where any needs related to money are unfulfilled. Even a man who is seeking alignment, who is starving for food, may find that it's fitting to kill or steal from another for food since his moral compass has been suppressed by hunger pains, justifications, and overall poor thinking.

Many people believe that financial security comes from earning a certain level of money; however, without financial literacy, the money earned isn't secure and remains vulnerable to be depleted. An easy example is the basketball player who earns millions of dollars while playing but is without adequate financial resources shortly after the end of the player's career.

When taking control over one's own finances, it's important to identify and measure the amount of money spent on all expenses. It is then important to determine which expenses are necessary for survival or an acceptable quality of life. After deciding what's necessary versus what is not, a budget should be put into place that allows for the allocation of money into a freedom fund of some sort, which requires a conscious decision to live beneath one's own means. Some people specifically save money for a rainy day, which I believe is sending the wrong intention into the universe. Saving for a rainy day invites a rainy day in my opinion.

I believe that it is wise to label your savings or your collection of assets with a title that represents a positive, progressive intention, such as a freedom fund, a wealth fund, or a life-time traveling fund. A person wouldn't save 10% of their income and put it into a cancer fund in the event that the person were ever diagnosed with cancer because the person wouldn't want to attract the energy that is likely to accompany the intention of saving money for possible cancer treatments. I believe that saving money specifically for a rainy day should be viewed with similar reasoning.

Assets & Liabilities

Another key element of financial literacy is

understanding the difference between assets and liabilities beyond what is taught in college accounting classes. Being a student of Robert Kiyosaki's writings during my youth, I view an asset as something that has a reasonable chance to increase in value and/or provide passive or portfolio income. Owning a duplex that produces rental income and receiving book royalties are examples of passive income. The great thing about passive income is that it can be earned from multiple places at the same time, including while you are sleeping. An example of portfolio income would be receiving dividends, or distributions, from a public stock or a private company that you own.

Opposite of an asset, a liability is something that requires money from you. Your credit card debt, student loans, mortgages on primary residences, rent, and car loans are all liabilities. Many people thought that their primary residences were assets until the financial crisis hit and people found themselves owing more on their homes than they were worth. Although a primary residence can prove itself to have been an asset after selling for a profit, it would have been a liability the entire holding period.

Investing Versus Saving

When a person's savings are left under a mattress, in a safe, or in a savings account, it is positioned in an environment that is not conducive to creating generational wealth. Although it is prudent to save money, it is also wise to allocate a portion of your assets to invest in businesses, real estate, or income-producing intellectual property, such as book copyrights and music publishing. Currently, most savings accounts pay interest at a rate that is lower than the rate of inflation, which causes the purchasing power of the dollar to decline.

On the other hand, money invested wisely has the potential to grow and create generational wealth, mainly due to the power of compounding. Let's examine the power of compounding assuming that an investor takes the time to learn to trade and invest wisely: If an investor makes a one-time investment of $3,000.00 into a Roth IRA and achieves an average rate of return of 15% by buying the technology sector exchange-traded fund (XLK), reinvesting the dividends, and buying more shares during bear markets (drops in the market of at least 20%), in 30 years the $3,000.000 investment would be worth at least

$200,000.00. If the investor can grow the account at an average rate of 20%, the $3,000.00 investment grows to over $700,000.00 in 30 years. Now imagine if you were to invest $3,000.00 every year, reinvest the dividends, and buy more shares during every bear market. You can quickly see how wealth can be obtained, secured, and passed down for the utilization of future generations.

Buying & Creating Assets

There's a common saying that the rich buys assets and that the poor and middle class often spend their money on liabilities and other junk. This is often true. Many rich people have learned, or are instructed by advisors, to value money and to treat it with the utmost respect. The way to respect money is to spend it wisely and to place it in a situation where it acts as an employee and also an environment that is conducive to creating generational wealth.

What's not commonly discussed is that many rich people also know the importance of creating assets whenever possible. It typically takes money, or credit, to buy assets and many people without any real wealth have a hard time buying any substantial assets due to their financial limitations. However, many of the poorest people in the country are great writers and have the capacity to write best-selling books or pen hit songs. Many other poor people are exceptional artists who can paint or otherwise design breathtaking and value appreciating artwork. There is a long list of assets that can be exchanged for wealth that can be created with little to no money.

A key to maximizing your ability to create assets is the practice of immediately recording your ideas either on paper or in your phone. Ideas are the seeds to great wealth and they are not to be trusted to memory. Please record them immediately. If you are driving and are unable to use voice command to record your idea safely, please pull over as soon as safely possible and record your idea. Many times the answers to our prayers are delivered in the form of ideas that must be executed.

Purpose & Alignment

Two of the most powerful words in the universe, in my opinion, are purpose and alignment. Your purpose encompasses the work you are here to complete and is likely to vary depending on the stage of life. Alignment is the process of aligning with not only natural law but also aligning with one's true and divine purpose. Many people work jobs for money that are completely unrelated to the person's purpose, which often leads to a person who is unfulfilled and ultimately unhappy.

After making a persistent effort to align with the universe and natural law, a person's reason for existence often becomes known and the path that is to be traveled is often made clear. Although investing in businesses, real estate, and intellectual property are key cornerstones of creating generational wealth, I believe that the best investment that a person can make, especially for a person who is aware of his or her purpose, is in personal development and a business related to carrying out that purpose. **We all have within us something that is unique to each individual that can add value to a large number of people in the world.** Carrying out and monetizing your purpose is likely to lead to more wealth and happiness than any other avenue.

It is important to set the proper intention of seeking purpose alignment in lieu of dream chasing. The problem with dream chasing is that in many cases we have no way of knowing where the dream came from. Similar to other conditioning of the world, many people's dreams come from television, music, our parents, and other sources not in alignment with our purpose. However, purpose alignment is divine and seeking it over a dream is prudent and a good use of free will.

Generational Wealth: Beginner's Business & Investing Guide, 3rd Edition

For an abundance of tips for gaining generational wealth, including an in-depth explanation of stocks, real estate, mortgages, economics, and entrepreneurship, please read my book *Generational Wealth: Beginner's Business & Investing Guide, 3rd Edition.* The book is available on Amazon and signed copies are available at GWSigned.com.

BONUS

10 TIPS FOR FINANCIAL PROSPERITY

My mission is to help eradicate both financial and spiritual illiteracy and to empower the masses by making them aware of their power and responsibility as alchemists and co-creators. Although I believe that an innerstanding of the spiritual principles that constitute reality can begin to heal communities, I am also aware that many people who are without financial security often lack the capacity to have faith in the spiritual. This dynamic often creates an environment where moral compasses are suppressed and principles, or codes of ethics, are suspended.

I believe that my approach to healing communities and families by integrating financial and spiritual concerns is the wave of the future as more teachers will recognize the downside of addressing the spiritual without addressing the financial and of improving the financial without considering the impact of spiritual principles on the lives of clients. Following is a list of 10 financial tips designed to either begin or accelerate the path to financial independence and generational wealth.

1. "Gold labors diligently and contentedly for the wise owner who finds for it profitable employment, multiplying even as the flocks of the field." – *The Richest Man in Babylon*

2. Although jobs serve an important purpose in our society, they are not a viable long-term solution to the problems faced by those seeking financial independence and generational wealth. A job should be used to develop your work ethic, master your craft, and save money to start your own venture.

3. Forming a limited liability company to either build a business or to act as an investment holding company to protect assets from creditors is sound risk management.

4. A Roth IRA should be used for those with employment income to ensure tax-free income in retirement. Assets in a Roth IRA grow tax deferred and can be withdrawn during retirement, after age 59 ½, tax free.

5. Equity crowdfunding opportunities, such as those listed on Wefunder.com, should be considered when allocating investment assets. Although large, multi-national companies typically have the smallest chance of failure, startups with proven product-market fit and fast growing sales create better opportunities for generating astronomical ROI (return on investment).

6. Privately owned businesses, stocks, real estate, and intellectual property that can by monetized, such as books or music publishing, are the foundations of generational wealth.

7. It is important to track expenses, create a budget, and intentionally live beneath one's own means. Discretionary income should be used to invest in assets, such as stocks and real estate. However, for the man or woman aware of his or her purpose, the best investment is in your purpose.

8. Building and managing your credit profile creates the opportunity to use OPM (other people's money) and build wealth at an

accelerated pace.

9. Term life insurance from reputable organizations should be considered to reduce the chance of economic catastrophe in the event of loss of life to key earners or contributors.

10. The best companies and real estate in the world can make bad investments if purchased at horrible valuations. Valuation is key, especially when expecting prolonged holding periods. Buying quality assets, such as stocks and real estate, during recessions and bear markets improves long-term returns exponentially. Although buying assets during economic expansions can be prudent as well, the valuations are usually not nearly as reasonable as when people are panicking during temporary downturns.

REFERENCED & RECOMMENDED READING

AFRIKA, LLAILA (2009). *MELANIN: WHAT MAKES BLACK PEOPLE BLACK!*

CLASON, GEORGE S. (1926). *THE RICHEST MAN IN BABYLON*

LAGERQUIST, KAY, & LENARD, LISA (2004). *THE COMPLETE IDIOT'S GUIDE TO NUMEROLOGY (2ND ED.)*

RUIZ, DON MIGUEL (1997). *THE FOUR AGREEMENTS: A PRACTICAL GUIDE TO PERSONAL FREEDOM*

SILVERSTONE, ALICIA (2011). *THE KIND DIET: A SIMPLE GUIDE TO FEELING GREAT, LOSING WEIGHT, AND SAVING THE PLANET*

THREE INITIATES (2012). *THE KYBALION: A STUDY OF THE HERMETIC PHILOSOPHY OF ANCIENT EGYPT AND GREECE*

ABOUT THE AUTHOR

LaFoy Orlando Thomas III, Esq. is an American attorney, entrepreneur, and investor. He earned his law degree from the University of Arkansas School of Law in Fayetteville, Arkansas. LaFoy has previously been licensed as a financial advisor, and his experience also includes management, mortgage lending, and real estate investing. He has been featured by various media outlets, including Business Insider. LaFoy is also an avid vegan and is the founder of the Trap Vegan clothing brand.

LaFoy is determined to share his wealth of both financial and, more importantly, spiritual wisdom with the masses and contribute to eradicating both financial and spiritual illiteracy. The author's mission is to empower the masses by making them aware of their power and responsibility as alchemists and co-creators. In addition to the books already mentioned, LaFoy is also the author of *Life Wisdom for Young Adults: Tips for Happiness, Alignment, and Generational Wealth.*

Although LaFoy believes that an

innerstanding of the spiritual principles that constitute reality can begin to heal communities, he is also aware that many people who are without financial security often lack the capacity or desire to have faith in the spiritual. This dynamic often creates an environment where moral compasses are suppressed and principles, or codes of ethics, are suspended.

The author believes that his approach to healing communities and families by integrating financial and spiritual concerns is the wave of the future. He believes that more private teachers and coaches will soon recognize the downside of addressing the spiritual without addressing the financial and of improving the financial without considering the impact of spiritual principles on the lives of clients. To book a life-coaching session or a paid speaking engagement with LaFoy, please visit GWLifeCoaching.com. For a signed copy of his book, *Generational Wealth*, please visit GWSigned.com.

Made in the USA
Middletown, DE
07 November 2019

78128060R00071